TO GARRY

I lay here in bed, and corrected
your rhyme.
But now I'd like to take some
time
To tell you what I fell about
art:

It's not spelling or grammar, but
what's in your heart.
All of the feelings in the things
that you said
Makes me stop for a while
and get into your head.

That's the true purpose of poetry,
take it from me.
So, move over Shakespeare,
Make room for GZ!

Richard Keeling

LIFE CAN BE CRAZY

**POETRY:
IT'S THE WAY BACK TO SANITY**

M. GARRY ZAFRANI

Copyright © 2023 M. Garry Zafrani

All Rights Reserved
Printed in the United States of America 2023 First Edition

All rights reserved. Original poetry by M Garry Zafrani. No part of this publication may be reproduced, stored in a retrieval system, or transmitted in any form or by any means – for example, electronic, photocopy, recording – without prior written permission of the publisher. The only exception is brief quotations in printed reviews.

Cover credits: Background Photo, Mina Nakamura.
Design: Debra Hayes via Canva Pro, Canva.com

Hardback ISBN: 979-8-9880849-0-7
Ebook ISBN: 979-8-9880849-1-4

Debra Lynn, LLC

ABOUT THE AUTHOR

Born in Brooklyn in 1949, Garry Zafrani grew up in a working-class family. As soon as he could get out of his family's house, he moved to Manhattan, eager to explore the city's cultural scene. He quickly became part of many different cultural movements, including Doo Wop, Bohemians, Beatniks, and long-haired hippies. However, his life took a dramatic turn when he was drafted into the Vietnam War.

Garry faced many challenges throughout his life, from homelessness to drug addiction but he always managed to bounce back. Poetry was one of the main tools as he became a true survivor. This determination and resilience of his has inspired many people. Today, he is known as a true-blue New Yorker living it up in Florida, a brave Vietnam veteran, and a successful entrepreneur.

CONTENTS

TO GARRY i
ABOUT THE AUTHOR. v

BEGINNING. 1
ALONE 2
ONE. 3
BORED 4
INFATUATION. 6
THE POWER SHE HAS OVER ME. 7
NIGHT PEOPLE. 8
CONFUSION 9
I AM ME 10
EVE OF DEPRESSION. 11
LOVE. 12
VALENTINES DAY 1980 13
MY WOMAN 15
MY LITTLE PRECIOUS. 16
RELATIVITY. 17
WHERE? 18
SHOOT FOR THE STARS. 19

BEGINNING

My poetry is pitiful,
Self-pity more sublime.
I use this paper and this ink,
Just to alter time.

I find my life's a struggle,
In syncopated time.
Oh, to pick a course that sets me free
And lets my life be mine.

When all the people start to say
Your fun in life is through,
Do I scare and run away,
and have a fling or two?

My life's too short to waste that way,
And so, I say to you:
Having fun and being crazy
doesn't make a fool.
I set my stride to reach my goal,
fair price I am willing to pay,
Now to fine the one who'll ride,
And give comfort along the way.

My journey's all ready to hurt my pride;
Oh God, it's only the first day!

ALONE

Alone in a room, your ears really hear
sounds from within that are fuel for your fear.

Horrendous noises through the night.
To live with them is my plight.
Searching for the answers from where they come.
Knowing a few and guessing at some.

The boiler and train were easy for me.
The refrigerator though closer was harder to see.
Four more noises still to track down.
A clink, a vibration and two whistling sounds.

With the twenty sounds my room does make,
to know only sixteen seems a mistake.
A fight to the finish it looks to be.
My room and it's noises against only me.

ONE

I have to become one with the universe;
I have to fill myself again.

I have to become one with space and time;
I have to pace myself again.

I have to become one with my destiny;
I have to find myself again.

I have to become one with the world;
I have to not lose myself again.

BORED

If my life began at 12:01
Is it sad or lots of fun?

If I'm up at 12:02
Am I happy or feeling blue?

If I wait till 12:03
Am I with someone or just with me?

If I ease into 12:04
Will there be a knock on my door?

If I think at 12:05
Do I want to stay alive?

If I sigh at 12:06
It's cause it's me in this fix?

If I pray at 12:07
Let me die and go to heaven.

If I'm awake at 12:08
Do I sit and wait and wait?

If I see at 12:09
I'm all alone. Do I pine?

If this is my last verse,
The hour 12:10
then I'm breaking the point
on this fuckin' pen!

INFATUATION

Her loveliness astounds
me.
No move I dare to
make.

Her soul begins to crowd
me.
No step I dare to take.

Her presence keeps to hound
me.
No style I know to
fake.

Her right to be around
me.
No sense to know a
mistake.

THE POWER SHE HAS OVER ME

The power she has over me
should not be entrusted to a bitch.

For not knowing her capacity,
she could easily be a witch.

To let her learn her responsibility,
so I don't have to twitch.

And every time she needs a scratch
I will take away the itch.

So, open up that door to me.
Let me hear your pitch.

NIGHT PEOPLE

*My life starts at midnight,
to die every morning at dawn.
Life at night, no light in sight.
Oh, what a fright when lights first spawn.*

*To miss the light is my delight.
Still loving in the early morn.*

CONFUSION

Confusion burns very high;
it's a blazing fever.
But seeing theirs
helps make mine meeker.

Confusion is so easily caught;
it's very contagious.
But catching theirs
makes mine less outrageous.

Confusion is not a tangible;
it's manufactured by your brain.
But knowing they're all messed up
cases all the pain.

Confusion is a wild bird;
it's free to roam.
But finding that it's not just me
doesn't get me home.

Confusion is a war game;
it should be stopped from within.
But I need answers,
so open up, that I might win.

I AM ME

I am me, and always will be!
But is that really a fact?

I am me, but not really free.
That tool called money sees to that.

I am me, and really do see
That living is where it's at.

I am me, so money will flee'
Unless I decide to change my act.

I am me, but do I sacrifice he,
Just to own a Cadillac?

I am me, loving life's spree.
A pauper passing the hat.

EVE OF DEPRESSION

Where has all the fury gone? Direction and purpose fade in my mind as the green of the seas fades with the setting sun. I used to follow that sun, now I wait for the sunrise and find it's the longest night of my life.

Where has all the motivation gone? A child's curiosity and competitiveness always fascinated me. I saw myself relating to that drive like a sleek and shiny jet relates to a single propeller plane.

Where have all the special people gone? Like a black and white TV set, I get used once in a while when the color set is on the blink. As soon as it gets fixed, I go back into the closet.

Where has the Garry, the "I can do anything!" gone? I think I'm drowning in a pool of lazy self-pity. My friends are like twigs that can me up for a while. But what or who will be the tree to lower one branch for me to get myself out with? My search for that tree is a Catch-22. It slides me deeper into my pool.

God, help me!

LOVE

To be so together,
To be so confused.
What pleasure to share.
What pain to bear.

A beautiful life to live for.
Living a slow death for sure.
A need that's hard to shake.
A vice that squeezes till you break.

Days never more perfect.
Nights ever so lonely.
That perfect strange magic.
Life as weak as a drug addict.

So very hard to find.
So easily lost.
The pot at the end of the rainbow.

Love: is like bring used by a nymph like a dildo.

VALENTINES DAY 1980

The ways that I miss you
cannot be described.
But to give you an idea
I'm going to try.

The ocean moves.
Cause of things life the tide.
The moon and its gravity
take the ocean for a ride.

You, like the moon
have a power I can't see.
A love that is real
and allows me to be free.

Like the soil on the ground
homes the roots of the trees.
Your love is my home
and takes care of my needs.

Being without you
feels lonely and bad.
It makes me appreciate
the good times we've had.

Soon I will see you
and we will be all alone.
Like the roots of the tree
I'll know that I'm home.

HAPPY VALENTINES DAY!

MY WOMAN

A body needs a certain warmth.
My woman sleeps beside me.

A person needs a certain thought.
My woman knows to guide me.

A someone needs a certain word.
My woman knows to thank me.

A being needs a certain place.
My woman shares her bed with me.

A mind needs a certain game.
My woman sits and plays with me.

A body needs a certain warmth.
My woman stays with me.

MY LITTLE PRECIOUS

My precious is honest,
and not scared to be free.
Knowing a bird on the wing,
still needs a good tree.

She and I have some things
we must do.
Like working and partying
and going to school.

I see us making small circles
in time.
Mine touching hers,
and hers touching mine.

But the time we're apart,
Is worth it you see.
It builds love in the hearts,
Of my precious and me.

RELATIVITY

The word is relativity, in
that it makes it count.
If it's good all the time,
then there's something to worry about.

So, I try not to let it bother me,
those problems that come my way.
For I'm 29 and still a child,
so, I'll handle them day by day.

Good problems make great accomplishments.
Of this I'm pretty sure.
Without hardships that come in life,
the good times would be relatively poor.

WHERE?

To find life I have look in places,
Only to lose myself in complacent atmospheres.

To find friends I have given of myself,
Only to see friends have no obligation.

To find peace, I have drugged my body,
Only to relax through the eye of the chemical.

To find strength, I have strained my bones,
Only to realize the strain has weakened me.

To find security, I have walled with thoughts,
Only to have it torn down like tissue paper.

To find love, I have met the people,
Only to find it comes to me when I least expected.

To find myself, I have looked,
Only to see I'm right here.

SHOOT FOR THE STARS

I need a new life, I used to say.
To be something larger than a fat man at play.

So change my goals was the next thing to do.
My body, my home, my head and the crew.

Two homes later, I'm here to stay.
Good days, bad days, and lots of pounds along the way.

My thoughts are better, this I can see.
The new friends around me are kind as can be.

My advice to you from what I've seen with my eye
is if you're unhappy with who you are....

Change it!
And always shoot for the sky!

www.ingramcontent.com/pod-product-compliance
Lightning Source LLC
Chambersburg PA
CBHW020333010526
44119CB00002B/45